Tornadoes

William B. Rice

Tornadoes

Publishing Credits

Associate Editors
James Anderson
Torrey Maloof

Editorial Director
Dona Herweck Rice

Editor-in-Chief
Sharon Coan, M.S.Ed.

Creative Director
Lee Aucoin

Illustration Manager
Timothy J. Bradley

Publisher
Rachelle Cracchiolo, M.S.Ed.

Science Consultant
Scot Oschman, Ph.D.

Teacher Created Materials
5301 Oceanus Drive
Huntington Beach, CA 92649-1030
http://www.tcmpub.com

ISBN 978-1-4333-0311-1

Table of Contents

Here It Comes!

The sky becomes gray and then nearly black before it turns a strange, sickly green. The howling wind blows with a mighty whip. Rain falls in a violent downpour, and hailstones strike the land. Leaves and **debris** on the land are tossed across the ground and into the air. A whirling gray funnel can be seen, reaching from the sky down to the ground. It roars like a freight train as it rips across the land. Branches crack and whole trees uproot. Everything not tied down is pushed or tossed by the powerful wind. Even things that are secure are tossed and hurled. Brick walls may tumble and windows may shatter. Buildings may even blow to the ground and scatter into pieces.

Through the turmoil, sirens blast and wail. They are the town's emergency warning. A **tornado** is here!

Everyone must run for cover to a basement or other safe shelter as soon as the warning comes. A tornado can be one of the fiercest and most powerful storms of all.

A tornado is transparent. We see it because it picks up dust or debris, or a cloud forms in the funnel.

How Many?

Each year, there are thousands of tornadoes around the world.

What Makes a Tornado?

A tornado is a fast and dangerous spinning column of air with a downward **funnel** cloud. The cloud acts like a vacuum when it touches the ground. It moves across the ground at speeds of about 50 kilometers (30 miles) per hour.

Scientists do not know exactly why a tornado forms. But they do know the weather conditions that make it happen. They are **moisture**, heat, and **lift**.

Most people have seen a thunderstorm. A thunderstorm is made of thunder and lightning. It often includes rain, but not always. Tornadoes usually happen in thunderstorms. Thunderstorms can form into **supercells**. A supercell is a very large thunderstorm that **rotates**. To rotate is to spin in a circle.

A mother and child run to a safe place.

Stay Put and Stay Safe

You cannot outrun a tornado, so it is best to get to a safe place fast when a tornado is on the way.

Watch Out!

Tornadoes can occur in a series, one after the other. One supercell may create several tornadoes.

The arrow in this satellite photo of a supercell shows the location of a new tornado.

A tornado forms from a supercell.

What Is It?

The **atmosphere** is the mass of gases (air) surrounding the Earth, or another body in space.

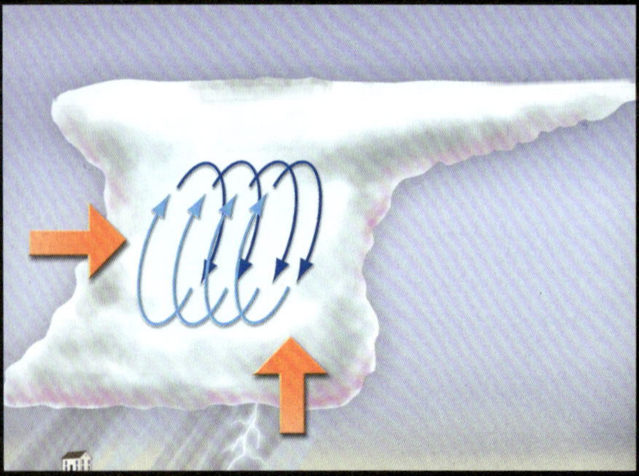

A thunderstorm can develop a supercell inside it. Winds go up, over, down, and back in a circle.

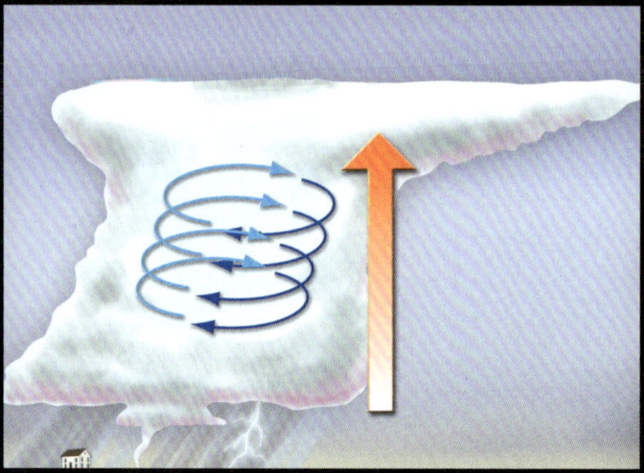

The supercell can get tilted up and down by a strong updraft.

Supercells rotate because of winds. Powerful winds of different temperatures meet. They come from different levels of the atmosphere. If they meet in the right way with enough strength, they turn the storm like a top. This makes a strong **updraft**. The updraft moves the supercell upward. It becomes a tornado when this rotating storm reaches its funnel to the ground. It can suck up wind and everything else it meets into the cell, as a vacuum would.

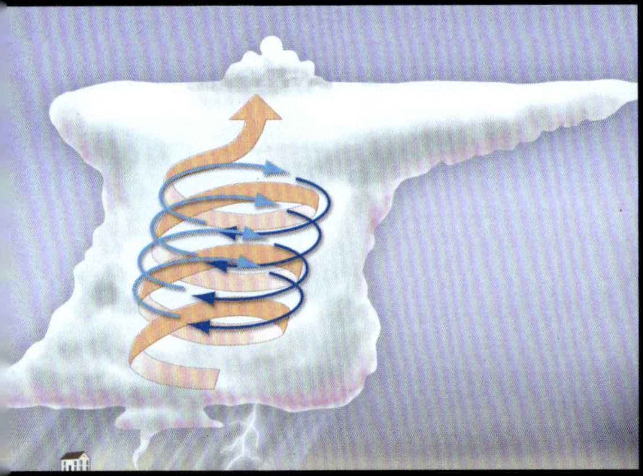

If the vertical supercell keeps going, it starts sucking wind and everything else up the cell. A tornado is born.

How Big and How Fast?

Tornadoes are usually less than 500 meters (1,640 feet) wide. They can be as wide as 1.5 kilometers (.9 miles). Winds can move up to about 500 kilometers (more than 300 miles) per hour. Tornadoes usually last just a few minutes, but they can last more than an hour.

But what exactly makes the winds in the first place? The sun is the cause. The sun heats the Earth, but everything is not heated evenly. The warmer the ground, the more it heats the air above it. This warm air rises. As it rises, cooler air floods below it. If the warm air rises quickly, the cooler air rushes in quickly, too. This is the wind.

As the warm air rises, it begins to cool. When it cools, it falls. Then it rushes in to take the place of warm air that is rising. In this way, the cycle of wind continues. It may be that the cycle creates only a gentle breeze. But it may also create a fierce and powerful tornado.

That's Powerful!

A tornado's winds are so strong that they can drive a piece of straw into wood as though it were a nail. It can also drive wood into metal. In this image, a golf club has been driven by a tornado through a thick kitchen door!

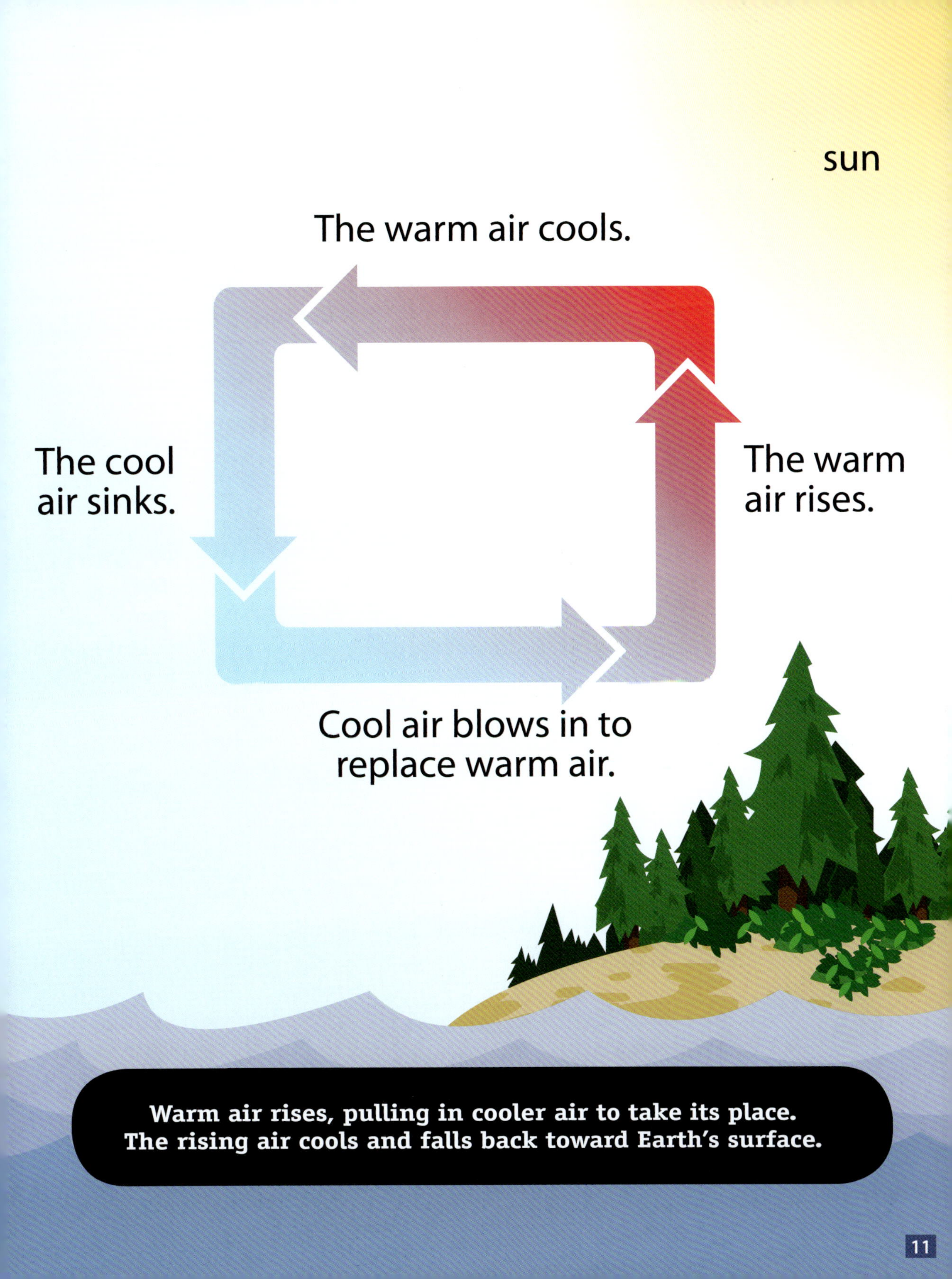

Warm air rises, pulling in cooler air to take its place. The rising air cools and falls back toward Earth's surface.

Most wind is fairly calm and even pleasant for people. Everyone enjoys a cool breeze on a warm day. But big winds can be terrifying because of the damage they may do.

T. Theodore Fujita made the **Fujita Tornado Scale** in 1970. It rates the wind's strength by speed and possible effects.

Fujita Tornado Scale

F0

less than 117 kph
(73 mph)

Light damage
chimneys damaged, branches broken, shallow-rooted trees pushed over, signs damaged

F1

117–180 kph
(73–112 mph)

Moderate damage
surface of roofs peeled, mobile homes pushed over, moving cars pushed off roads

F2

181–253 kph
(113–157 mph)

Considerable damage
roofs torn from houses, mobile homes destroyed, large trees uprooted, cars lifted off ground and thrown

T. Theodore Fujita

The true wind speeds of tornadoes are not known. These speeds are estimates. The damage a wind does at a certain speed will vary from place to place. So the Fujita Scale rates a tornado and its speed based on the damage that it causes.

F3

254–332 kph
(158–206 mph)

Severe damage

walls torn off well-made houses, trains overturned, most trees uprooted, heavy cars lifted off ground and thrown

F4

333–418 kph
(207–260 mph)

Devastating damage

well-made houses destroyed, structures blown away some distance, cars thrown like missiles

F5

419–512 kph
(261–318 mph)

Incredible damage

strong frame houses leveled and blown away, cars thrown through the air more than 100 meters (109 yards), trees stripped of bark

Twisting the Night Away

In the United States on April 3-4, 1974, 148 tornadoes struck 13 states in 16 hours. That is the worst-known series of tornadoes on record anywhere. More than 300 people were killed, more than 5,000 people were injured, and thousands of miles of land and property were damaged.

Where Do Tornadoes Happen?

Tornadoes can happen anywhere in the world. But they are common in just a few places. They are quite uncommon in others. For example, scientists agree that a tornado in Antarctica is unlikely. The temperature and lack of moisture prevent it. But other places have just the right conditions. Tornadoes happen there all the time.

Most tornadoes happen in **"Tornado Alley."** This is an area that stretches through the Great Plains of the United States. It reaches from South Dakota through Texas. But tornadoes can happen wherever there is a fierce thunderstorm. Australia sees many tornadoes each year. So do Canada and South Africa. China and India do, too.

Danger Zone

Most tornadoes in the world happen in Tornado Alley. Many scientists believe that tornadoes occur there when warm, moist air from the Gulf of Mexico meets cool, dry air from Canada.

Tornadoes are common in Tornado Alley for one big reason. Tornado Alley has a lot of everything a storm needs to become a tornado. What does it have? Heat, moisture, and lift.

The heat throughout Tornado Alley comes from the sun. The moisture comes mainly from the Gulf of Mexico. And the lift comes from a dry line of air that meets moist air from another direction. These things together are a winning combination when it comes to making tornadoes.

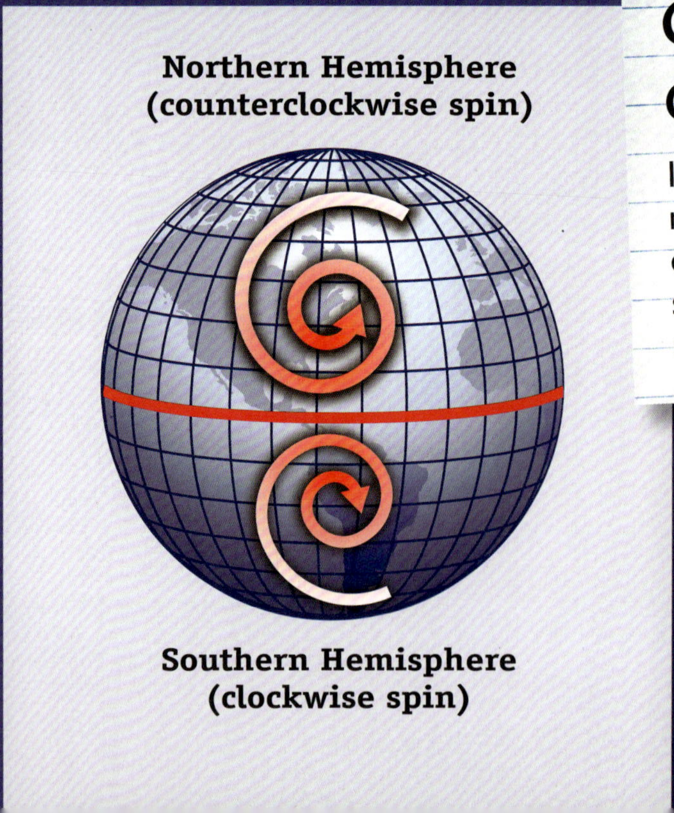

Clockwise or Counter?

In the northern hemisphere, most tornadoes spin counterclockwise. In the southern hemisphere, they mainly spin clockwise.

Twister

A tornado is also called a twister. That is because the wind "twists" as the cloud spins.

Once a tornado strikes, no one knows where it will go. And no one can predict where it will strike. Even with the right conditions, a tornado may not happen. But it may happen suddenly and as a surprise to everyone.

A tornado may follow a steady path. But it may easily shift direction and move away from where it was headed. It may even move through a street in a town, wiping out houses on one side of the street and barely touching houses on the other side. It is nearly impossible to know what a tornado will do once it has begun.

Waterspouts

When a tornado occurs over water, it is called a **waterspout**. It forms when warm, moist air lifts rapidly over water. It becomes a column of water over the ocean or a lake. Just as a tornado sucks up air and other things, a waterspout sucks up water and other things. It can even lift fish, carry them away, and drop them onto land.

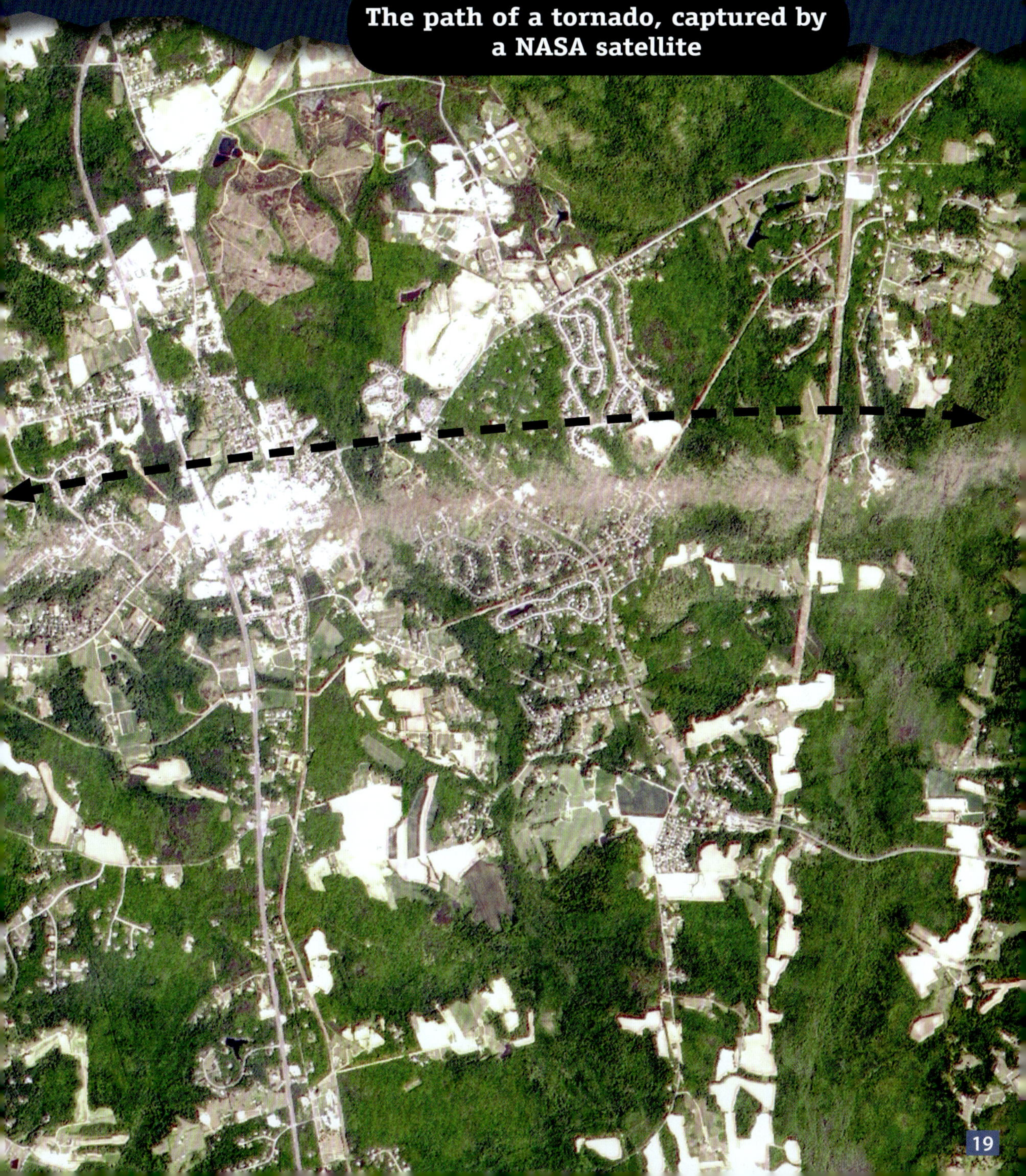

The path of a tornado, captured by a NASA satellite

Dust Devils

A dust devil looks like a small tornado, but it is not one. It is a whirling wind of dust, dirt, and other debris. This dust devil is in Africa.

Stages of a Tornado

beginning

funnel stage

mature stage

After a Tornado

Tornadoes are powerful. They can be frightening, too. But they do not last forever. A tornado begins when a funnel from a cloud reaches the land and travels across the ground. As it does, it loses its strength. Its energy begins to fade. Finally, the funnel shrinks away. It goes back into the cloud. And that is the end of the tornado.

After a storm like this, it is strange to imagine clear skies. But that is usually what happens when a tornado ends. The sky is clear and calm.

end

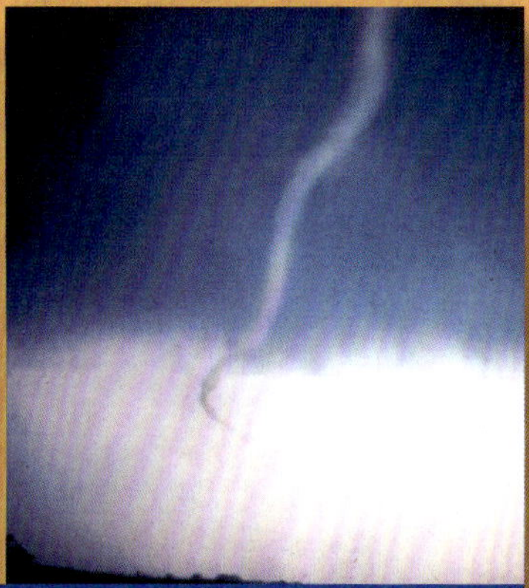

rope stage

When the tornado fades, it is not just a memory. It leaves great destruction behind.

At its best, a tornado strikes in areas where people do not live. There, it might rip up trees and throw rocks and other debris. But no one is injured. At its worst, a tornado strikes where many people live. Windows are shattered and roofs are blown away. Cars are thrown through the air. Power lines are knocked down. Homes and buildings are destroyed. People and animals are injured and killed.

The path of a tornado is narrow. But a tornado is such a powerful storm that its damage can be broad. After a tornado, it can take a very long time to make things right again.

Worst Tornado Ever

More than 500,000 people were killed in 1970 when a powerful tornado struck an area that is now Bangladesh.

What to Do

When a tornado strikes, people must take cover. When they think a tornado is coming, people bring patio furniture, toys, and other loose items inside. They go into storm shelters below ground or into rooms and hallways that do not have windows or outside doors. It is important to stay safe inside shelters.

a storm shelter

tornado damage

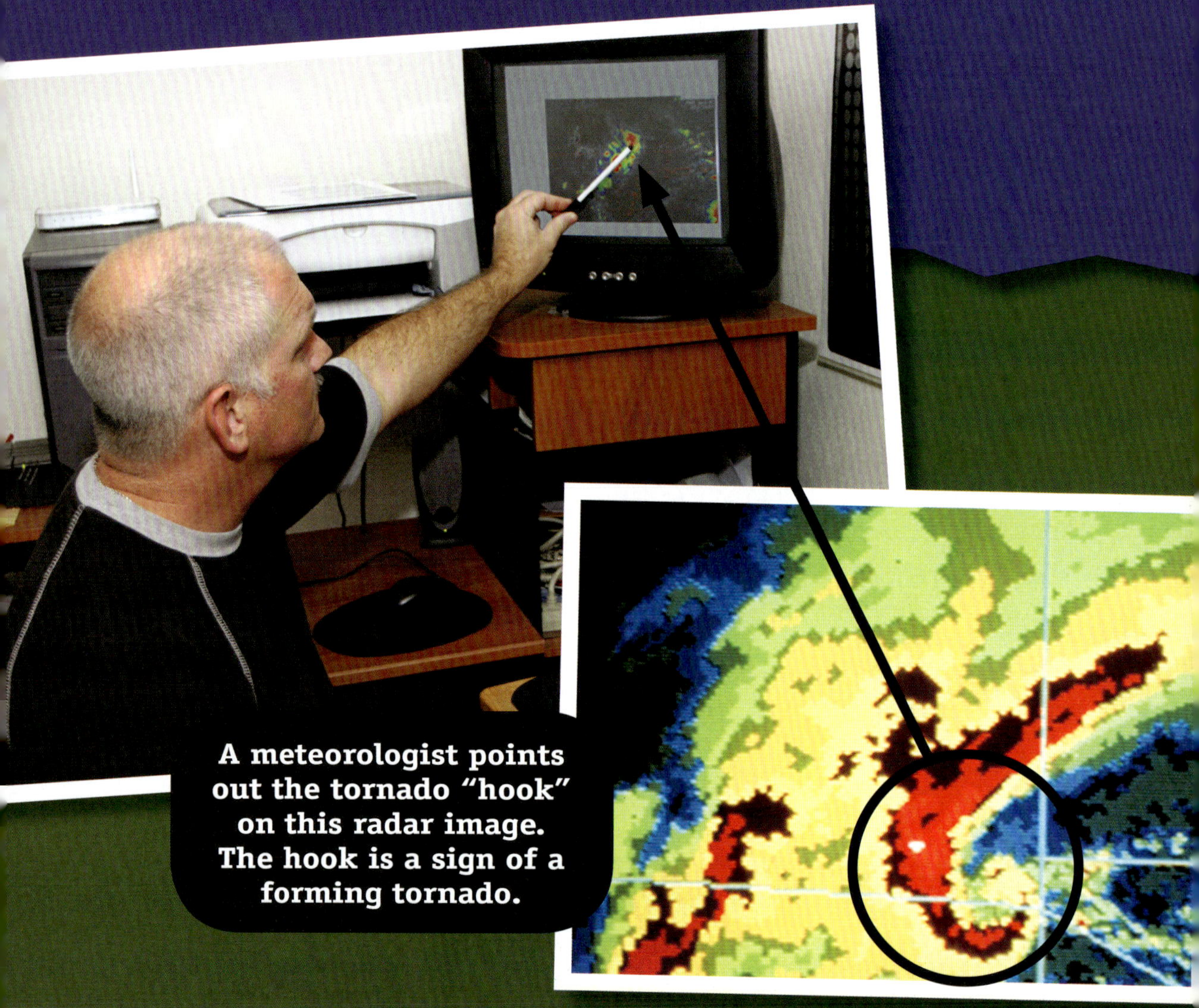

A meteorologist points out the tornado "hook" on this radar image. The hook is a sign of a forming tornado.

In the past, people had a hard time being prepared for a tornado. They had no way of knowing when and where it would strike. Not long ago, **meteorologists** (mee-tee-uh-ROL-uh-jists) needed to see the tornados before they could issue a warning. Now, there is new technology. Meteorologists can watch storms as they form. They can issue warnings with about 11 minutes lead time. Those 11 minutes can make all the difference. Getting warnings to people ahead of time may not prevent a lot of future damage. But it will help to keep many more people safe.

Storm Chasers

Not everyone runs for shelter in a storm. Storm chasers do just the opposite. They want to learn all about tornadoes. So they follow storms, hoping to come close to a tornado and study it. This is very dangerous. But the more they can learn, the better we can predict tornadoes in the future.

A Russian meteorologist takes measurements in the field.

Mobile labs gather supercell storm data in Kansas.

An Indonesian meteorologist studies satellite-photo data.

Can a Tornado Be Stopped?

Scientists through history have tried to find a way to stop tornadoes. Tornadoes can do much damage. People would like to quiet them quickly or stop them from forming in the first place.

Scientists have had many ideas. Some have thought that dry ice thrown into the storm might end a tornado. But it would be nearly impossible to get the ice to the right spot. It wouldn't likely do much good anyway. Some have even thought about setting a bomb to stop a tornado! But a bomb may cause more damage than the tornado itself.

The truth is that even if we could stop one tornado, the storm would probably just create another one. Thunderstorms are powerful things. They are even more powerful than the tornadoes they create.

Stopping a tornado is unlikely. The better use of time for scientists is learning about why, how, and where tornadoes form. The sooner they can predict a tornado, the safer everyone is. And that is the most important thing.

Lab: Twister in a Bottle

To see what happens when a funnel is created in a tornado or hurricane, try this experiment. Watch carefully and take some notes about what you see.

Materials

- two plastic bottles
- duct tape
- water

Procedure:

1. Fill one of the bottles about half to three-fourths full with water.
2. Place the open ends of the two bottles together, neck to neck.
3. Securely tape the two necks together by wrapping duct tape around them. Wrap the tape so that it is flat and neat.
4. Turn the bottles over and swirl them so that the water spins through the openings, creating a whirlpool.
5. Watch what happens. What does it tell you about tornadoes and hurricanes?

1

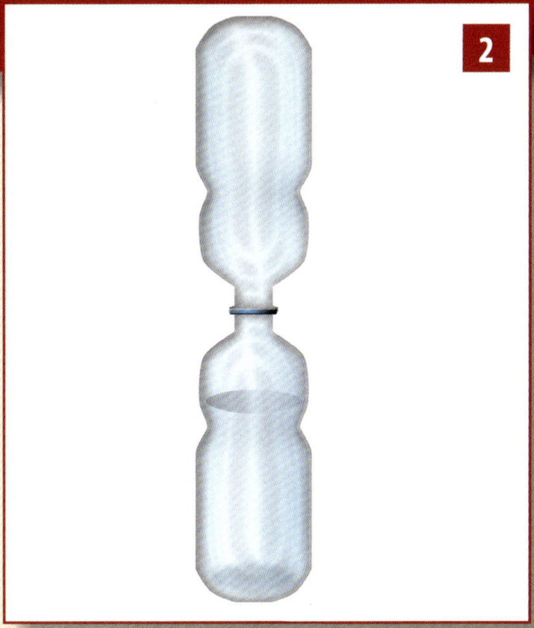
2

3

4

Glossary

atmosphere—the mass of gases surrounding the Earth, or another body in space

debris—loose waste material

Fujita Tornado Scale—a rating scale developed in 1970 by the scientist T. Theodore Fujita to categorize tornadoes and their relative strength

funnel—a hollow cone open on both ends

lift—the force that raises something up

meteorologist—weather scientist

moisture—wetness

rotate—move in a circle

supercell—a rotating thunderstorm

tornado—a destructive windstorm with a funnel-shaped cloud that extends to the ground

Tornado Alley—an area of North America that experiences hundreds of tornadoes each year

updraft—air movement upwards

waterspout—a tornado over the ocean or a lake that sucks up water

Index

Scientists Then and Now

John Dalton
(1766–1844)

John Dalton is best known for studying atoms. But he also studied weather. He kept a daily journal about the weather patterns in his town from 1787 until 1844! He even used homemade equipment to measure the weather. Many believe it was Dalton's journal that helped bring about the scientific study of weather known today as meteorology.

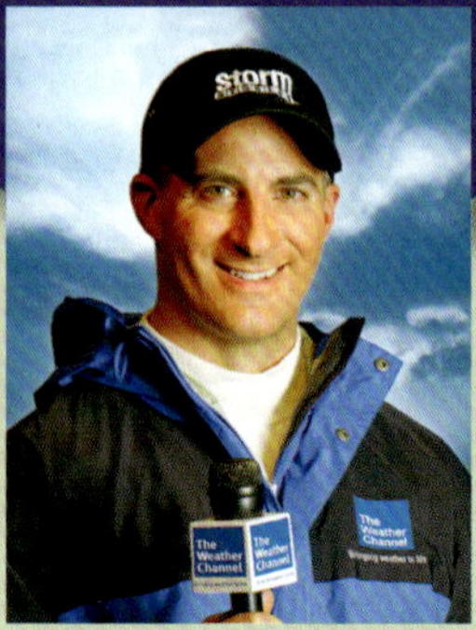

Jim Cantore
(1964–)

Jim Cantore is a meteorologist for The Weather Channel. He has been studying the weather since he was a boy. Cantore's classmates used to call him and ask him to predict the weather! Today, he predicts the weather for people all over the world. He helps keep people safe by telling them when and where the next storm will hit.

Image Credits

Cover Newscom; p.1 Newscom; p.4 Michal Strzelecki/Shutterstock; p.4-5 Gregor Kervina/Shutterstock; p.6 Mike Agliolo/Photo Researchers, Inc.; p.6-7 A. T. Willett/Alamy; p.7 NOAA; p.8-9 Tim Bradley; p.9 Tim Bradley; p.10 Jim Reed/Photo Researchers, Inc.; p.10-11 Stephanie Reid; p.12(left) Jonathan Lenz/Shutterstock; p.12(center) Slobodan Djajic/Shutterstock; p.12(right) Lilac Mountain/Shutterstock; p.13(left) Susan Law Cain/Shutterstock; p.13(center) Steve Byland/Shutterstock; p.13(right) Diana Lundin/Shutterstock; p.13(top) Courtesy of University of Chicago; p.14-15 Newscom; p.15 Tim Bradley; p.16 Stephanei Reid; p.16-17 Katherine Bay/Jim Reed Photography/Photo Researchers, Inc.; p.17(right) Joe Lertola; p.18 Dark o /Shutterstock; p.19 NASA; p.20-21 Kondrachov Vladimir/Shutterstock; p.20-21(bottom) Credit: NOAA Photo Library, NOAA Central Library; OAR/ERL/National Severe Storms Laboratory (NSSL); p.22 Harry Koundakjian/AP; p.22-23 Mike Theiss/Science Photo Library/Photo Researchers; p.23 Larry Miller/Photo Researchers, Inc.; p.24(left) Lisa F. Young/Shutterstock; p.24(right) NOAA; p.25 Mike Berger/Photo Researchers, Inc.; p.26(top left) Vladimir Sayapin/ITAR-TASS/Newscom; p.26(top right) Jim Reed/Photo Researchers, Inc.; p.26(bottom) Adek Berry/AFP/Newscom; p.28-29 Tim Bradley; p.32(left) Library of Congress; p.32(right) Courtesy of The Weather Channel, Inc.